# THE CALL OF THE PROPHETIC INTERCESSOR

# THE CALL OF THE

# PROPHETIC

# INTERCESSOR

TERRI ANDERSON

Designed by D' Technology

Published by D.O.R.M. International Publishing

A Christian Publisher located in Atlanta, Georgia (USA)

Visit our website at **www.dormpublishing.com**

Printed in the United States of America

First Edition: June 2022

ISBN-13: 978-1-957038-06-3

ISBN-10: 1-957038-06-3

D.O.R.M
PUBLISHING

# DEDICATION

This book is dedicated to all of those who know they have been called and chosen, to those who may have strayed away from that position and need to get back in place, and to those who are struggling and have been seeking God for answers to find your place concerning Him. As you read this book, I pray you will have a better understanding and clarity of the importance of your role in the ministry of prophetic intercession. In addition, you will be able to identify God's will and purpose for your life.

**May the God of love, peace, and prosperity be upon your life, in the mighty name of Jesus**

# TABLE OF CONTENTS

INTRODUCTION ........................................................................ 1

The Difference Between Prayer, Intercession, and Prophetic Intercession ........................................................................ 3

PRAYER ................................................................................ 5

What is Prayer? .................................................................. 6

What is the Purpose of Prayer? ........................................ 8

How do you Pray? .............................................................. 8

Types of Prayers ................................................................ 10

INTERCESSION ...................................................................... 13

What is intercession? ........................................................ 14

How do you Intercede? ...................................................... 16

What is an intercessor? ...................................................... 17

What is a Spiritual Gatekeeper? ...................................... 17

What is the role of the Spiritual Gatekeeper? ................ 18

PROPHETIC INTERCESSION ................................................ 21

What is Prophetic Intercession? ...................................... 22

How do you Prophetically Intercede? ............................ 22

What is a Prophetic Intercessor? .................................... 23

What is the Spiritual Watchman? .................................... 24

What is the Role of the Spiritual Watchman? ................ 24

The Requirement .................................................................... 27

IDENTIFYING THE CALL .................................................... 29

How to Identify the Call to Prophetic Intercession? ...... 31

Spiritual Connection .......................................................... 31

Dreams ................................................................................ 31

Visions ..................................................................... 32

Personal Spiritual Encounters .............................. 32

SURRENDERING TO THE CALL ............................... 35

Humility ................................................................ 36

Repentance ............................................................ 36

Purging and Purification ....................................... 37

DEVELOPING THE PROPHETIC INTERCESSOR ............... 39

Personal Relationship ........................................... 40

Understanding the voice of God ........................... 41

Prayer, Meditation, Fasting, and Studying the Word of God
............................................................................... 44

Obedience ............................................................. 45

Cultivate the Fruit of the Spirit ............................. 45

HANDLING THE OPPOSITION WITH THE CALL ............. 55

Internal Spiritual Warfare ..................................... 56

External Spiritual Warfare ..................................... 58

A MESSAGE TO THE PROPHETIC INTERCESSORS .............. 63

ABOUT THE AUTHOR ................................................. 67

# INTRODUCTION

### The Call of the Prophetic Intercessor to Intercession

There is a clarion call to come to a place of prayer and repentance, and we must heed the call. There is a crying out and a spare not, a weeping, a wailing and travailing of souls in the spirit realm to come and be reconciled back to God.

We as intercessors, prophetic intercessors, spiritual gatekeepers and spiritual watchmen must have a lifestyle dedicated to prayer and fasting where we are praying without ceasing according to 1 Thessalonians 5:17 so that we will be able to hear from God earnestly and with clarity to release the word of God and operate in the call effectively in obedience. We will do this by yielding to His will and to His way in humble submission in order to overcome the enemy of darkness and spiritual wickedness in this world. We must be sold out to prayer.

*Prophetess Terri O. Anderson*

*"And He saw that there was no man, and wondered that there was no intercessor; therefore, His arm brought salvation unto him, and his righteousness, it sustained him."*

ISAIAH 59:16

# The Difference Between Prayer, Intercession, and Prophetic Intercession

# CHAPTER 1

## PRAYER

## What is Prayer?

Prayer is the spiritual communication between God and man. As He speaks to us, we talk to Him and wait for the results to happen.

Growing up as a little girl with my other three siblings and both of my parents, prayer and faith were the foundation of our family. My father and mother taught me the value and the importance of prayer. It all started at the dinner table by saying my grace and my bedtime prayers. I learned the fundamentals and the different principles of prayer as a child, which has carried me into my adulthood. It has helped me to overcome many challenges, many dangers seen and unseen, faith to do the impossible things, strength to endure, healing to my mind, body, and soul, deliverance, and restoration. It has also given me direction, led me to salvation for my soul, and I have found God's purpose for my life.

As a child, I **developed a speech impairment (stuttering),** something I inherited from my father. I went through speech therapy to help me through the process. I was mocked and teased growing up, but because of prayer, I survived through this challenging time of my life. I am an overcomer.

**A survivor of domestic abuse (in a relationship)** was a traumatic experience for me where I had to truly pray and ask God to give me the courage and the way of escape because I was tired. I wanted out. Through prayers and the support of my family, He delivered me and brought me out. I am a survivor.

**A survivor of a domestic crime (carjacked at gunpoint)** was a traumatic and frightening experience for me, not knowing if I was going to escape it with my life or die. I just know I was praying and calling on the name of "Jesus" while the incident was happening. He covered and protected me in the midst of danger and allowed me to escape. Glory to God!! Hallelujah. I am a survivor.

**A survivor of homelessness (with children)** being an independent single working mother of 2 sons and struggling on limited income to provide for my family was a challenging time for me. I begin to pray to the Lord about the situation even though He already knew. Sometimes we just have to go through the process in order to receive what he has for us. I am here to tell you because of prayer and faith and trying to live a consecrated life unto Him, my God!! my God!! I got a financial increase, and He opened 2 places for us to live. Then, I asked Him to help me to choose which one. I just thank Him for being a prayer answering God with the results you want and then much more. Glory to God!!! I am a survivor.

## What is the Purpose of Prayer?

The purpose is to help us open our hearts, our minds, and our souls to build a personal relationship with God. It helps to nurture and cultivate us in our character development and our spiritual growth process. It brings healing, deliverance, and restoration to our mind, body, and soul. It gives us guidance and direction for our lives and brings comfort in times of despair. It causes a supernatural change to transform our lives forever. Prayer destroys yokes. It breaks chains; it delivers man from the hand of the enemy and the strongholds in our lives so we can be free from bondage and self-will. We seek God through prayer to get in His will. *Read 2 Chronicles 7:14 GNT.*

## How do you Pray?

We can kneel, bow, laying prostrate, sit, stand, and walk around while we pray. Sometimes we pray in the gift of tongues, which is our (heavenly language). Sometimes we just pray in our regular language. We should always make sure our focus is on Him without any distractions. We are to pray in the

Spirit (because He is a spiritual being, not a fleshly being). His Spirit dwells within each of us, and this is how we communicate with Him, and we learn the truth about Him as He teaches us through prayer how He expects for us to live with the word of God abiding within us. He desires that we be sincere and earnest in our hearts; we are to acknowledge and reverence Him for who He is and for being our God and King {Elohim, Yahweh, El Shaddai, Adonai}.

We are to ask Him for forgiveness (Repent) for our wrongdoings and sinning against Him; we are to give Him thanks for everything He is doing, has done, and for what He is going to continue to do in our lives. We are to end our prayer with giving Him reverence with power and authority that we are trusting and believing that our prayers of petition are heard and granted according to our faith in His name (Jesus), amen. *Read Matthew 6:5-15 GNT.*

During our time of prayer and meditation with God is one way He does respond to us concerning our prayer request. Sometimes he responds immediately and other times He may respond to our request later. For instance, I was seeking answers and direction concerning my ministry, but He did not respond right away. I believed by faith He was going to direct me, so in the process He begin to align people in my path in order to fulfill my request. God will allow things to happen and situations and circumstances to come in your life. Sometimes He will give you a spoken word. He will even allow someone to speak a word in your life. Yes, He can answer our requests in different ways, but we must pay attention and listen when it is Him speaking in response.

## Types of Prayers

**Prayer of Adoration** is the opening prayer unto God with worship and reverence unto His word and for who He is in our lives. *Read Psalms 8:1*

**Prayer of Petition** is to ask for (request); to inquire of and to demand something from God. *Read 1 Timothy 2:1*

**Prayer of Repentance** is asking God for the forgiveness of all your sins; to ask for a change of mind; a change of heart for the salvation of your soul. *Read 2 Peter 3:9*

**Prayer of Thanksgiving** is giving a thanks offering; a confession; and a sacrifice of praise unto God for all He has done. *Read Leviticus 7:12*

**Prayer of Supplication** is when you plead the cause and ask God to show favor upon; to have mercy upon; to show pity to, on behalf of someone else in the time of trouble. *Read Psalms 6:9*

**Warfare Prayer** is when you are praying strategically under the influence of the Holy Spirit against the evil forces of this world: against principalities; against powers; rulers of darkness; spiritual wickedness in high places. *Read Ephesians 6:12*

# CHAPTER 2

# INTERCESSION

# What is intercession?

Intercession is when one is praying God's heart and pleading the cause of a situation or a matter on behalf of another as we read *Isaiah 53:10-12.*

> *"Yet, it pleased the LORD to bruise him; he hath put him to grief: when thou shalt make his soul an offering for sin, he shall see his seed, he shall prolong his days, and the pleasure of the LORD shall prosper in his hand. He shall see of the travail of his soul and shall be satisfied: by his knowledge shall my righteous servant justify many; for he shall bear their iniquities. Therefore, will I divide him a portion with the great, and he shall divide the spoil with the strong; because he hath poured out his soul unto death: and he was numbered with the transgressors; and he bare the sin of many, and made intercession for the transgressors."*

The above scripture is the theme God gave me in 2018 when He birthed **Woman of Travail Ministry International Prayer line.** The purpose of this ministry is to bring **Healing, Deliverance,** and **Restoration** and to **Birth Purpose** in the lives of the people through Intercessory Prayer and Worship. I teach and preach the Gospel of Christ so that those who are lost and don't know Him in the pardon of their sin will seek Him for salvation that is free to all. When we open up our hearts and allow Him to come in and have His way in our lives, a change begins to happen from the inside that will show on the outside. The call to Intercession that is upon my life today is great.

As a **prophetic intercessor,** I take this journey seriously because there is a crying out and a travailing of souls in the spiritual realm who need to come and be reconciled back to Christ and get healed, delivered, restored, and be set free from sin this is when we as (**intercessors**) are to stand in the gap on behalf of the transgressors.

**God Rescued and Delivered through Intercession**

"I had a great burden to begin to intercede for Oscar and I had been crying out in travail for his soul on the line because I had seen in the spirit that the enemy was trying to kill and destroy his life and destiny Why? It was because of the strongholds that he was battling with on the inside that caused him to be in the wrong place where darkness dwells. So, When I begin to pray strategically on his behalf, pulling down those strongholds in his life and disrupting the plots, the plans, and the schemes of the enemy and dispatching the angels on assignment to his life to go and fight on his behalf and warring against every demonic force against his life, My God!!!My God!! I am here to tell you that God not only rescued Oscar out of the enemy's camp, but He shut down the whole operation. What a mighty God we serve.

## How do you Intercede?

You start by giving Him reverence and thanks for who he is and for choosing you to intercede.

Ask Him for the forgiveness of your sins and remove it from your life so that your petitions won't be hindered.

Surrender your thoughts and your will. They may cause distractions.

Pray and ask God to plead the cause of every spoken request given by others under His power and authority.

Plead the blood over the situation or matter that it will be done in His name.

Welcome the Holy Spirit to come into your presence. We are to acknowledge and recognize Him as He is speaking, and we are listening to instructions. This is a time when we allow Him to communicate with us on how to pray and intercede for others in the spiritual realm so we can hear with clarity (being sensitive to the Holy Spirit).

> *"Likewise, the Spirit also helpeth our infirmities: for we know not what we should pray for as we ought: but the Spirit itself maketh intercession for us with groanings which cannot be uttered."*
>
> ROMANS 8:26

## What is an intercessor?

An **intercessor** (burden-bearer) is one who is called by God to stand in the gap and make up a hedge of protection and plead the cause on behalf of another. An intercessor reminds the Lord of His promises until they are fulfilled.

> *"O Israel, thy prophets are like the foxes in the deserts. Ye have not gone up into the gaps, neither made up the hedge for the house of Israel to stand in the battle in the day of the LORD."*
>
> EZEKIEL 13:4-5

## What is a Spiritual Gatekeeper?

A **spiritual gatekeeper** (porter) is one who is called and lives in the obedience of God who guards and protects the entry way of the heart, mind, and soul (temple of God) to not allow anything that is not like Him to come in that will cause disobedience (Sin).

> *"(for the weapons of our warfare are not carnal, but mighty through God to the pulling down of strong holds;) casting down imaginations, and every high thing that exalteth itself against the knowledge of God, and bringing into captivity every thought to the obedience of Christ; and having in a readiness to revenge all disobedience, when your obedience is fulfilled."*
>
> 2 CORINTHIANS 10:4-6

## What is the role of the Spiritual Gatekeeper?

The **spiritual gatekeeper** is to be in position at all times in prayer and obedience no matter what you have been called to do in this ministry, whether to teach the doctrine of Jesus Christ to the world and the nations; to preach the gospel of Jesus Christ to the world and nations; to usher God's people into His presence through worship and praise; to pray and intercede for the world and nations; to be the leader of your local church or even internationally.

You can be called to the governmental office, city, or county office. No matter what you are supposed to do in this hour and season, your needed in the Kingdom of God. The role of the spiritual gatekeeper is vital in this hour to help us gain access to the things of God in order to receive our breakthroughs. Those breakthroughs might be healing, deliverance, restoration, for spiritual growth and development, to see miracles, signs, and wonders manifest. No matter which is needed, it's time to stand guard and protect from all open portals (gates, entry way) from entering in our lives that will cause us to not come into divine alignment with Him.

# CHAPTER 3

# PROPHETIC
# INTERCESSION

## What is Prophetic Intercession?

Prophetic Intercession is a more intense form of prayer. It is when you prophetically hear and pray the heart and the will of God for the people *Read Job 22:27-28.*

## How do you Prophetically Intercede?

You acknowledge and reverence the Holy Spirit for who He is in your life.

Ask for forgiveness and repentance for all your sins and wrongdoings (Having a Godly sorrow), so it does not hinder your request during the time of prophetic intercession (must have a clear conscious of mind, no hidden secret sins).

You must open your heart to allow the Holy Spirit to come in and take complete and total control in you and through you. Allow him to search the debts of your heart and cleanse you from all unrighteousness (a purging) so a transformation (change) will begin to happen in you. We must be reconciled back to Him to walk in the Spirit of holiness and righteousness.

**As we read 2 Corinthians 5:17:**

*"Therefore, if any man be in Christ, he is a new*

*creature: old things are passed away; behold, all things are become new."*

We must be changed (transformed) as the scriptures speak to be in Christ, so we must live a life dedicated to prayer that causes change to happen within us in order to be set free from old things to become new in Christ.

## What is a Prophetic Intercessor?

A prophetic intercessor is someone who has been called to the ministry of the prophetic that hears and prays the voice and heart of God prophetically in the spiritual realm, who stands in the gap on behalf of others.

*And there was one Anna, a prophetess, the daughter of Phanuel, of the tribe of Aser: she was of a great age, and had lived with an husband seven years from her virginity; and she was a widow of about fourscore and four years, which departed not from the temple, but served God with fastings and prayers night and day. 38 And she coming in that instant gave thanks likewise unto the Lord, and spake of him to all them that looked for redemption in Jerusalem.*

**LUKE 2:36-37-38**

# What is the Spiritual Watchman?

The **spiritual watchman** (seer) is one who is called and lives in the obedience of God that sees and hears prophetically in the spiritual realm who is sent to bring warning to the people to turn from their wicked ways of sin and be delivered.

> *"So thou, O son of man, I have set thee a watchman unto the house of Israel; therefore, thou shalt hear the word at my mouth, and warn them from me. When I say unto the wicked, O wicked man, thou shalt surely die; if thou dost not speak to warn the wicked from his way, that wicked man shall die in his iniquity; but his blood will I require at thine hand. Nevertheless, if thou warn the wicked of his way to turn from it; if he do not turn from his way, he shall die in his iniquity; but thou hast delivered thy soul."*

Ezekiel 33:7-9

# What is the Role of the Spiritual Watchman?

The **spiritual watchman** is equipped by God to spiritually see and hear what others cannot through the spirit. They sound the alarm and give warning when there is an enemy in the midst that comes in disguise to cause conflict and confusion amongst the people. They are to guard and

24

protect the souls of the people from the wicked, one that comes to kill and destroy. They are to speak warning to those, whether it be individually or collectively.

When the watchman does not speak warning to the wicked to save their lives, and they die in their wickedness and sin, God holds the watchman accountable for the souls of those who were lost. As watchman, it's important you release the warnings of God so you will not have to encounter God's judgement for the souls of man. It's a watchman's responsibility to encourage the people, warn the people of God's judgement, and point them to repentance so they can be saved.

> *"And it came to pass at the end of seven days, that the word of the LORD came unto me, saying, 'Son of man, I have made thee a watchman unto the house of Israel: therefore, hear the word at my mouth, and give them warning from me.'*
>
> EZEKIEL 3:16-17

A spiritual watchman needs to always be in a position of prayer and obedience to the will of God, wherever and to whomever we have been assigned to. It can be your family, your church ministry, to the world and the nations, the workplace, the city; state; and local government, those in leadership, the children, the youth, the young adults, or the older adults. Your role is important in the Kingdom of God to guard and protect when necessary and to bring warning and correction to the lost and dying soul. You are God's prophetic mouthpiece that brings warning before destruction falls. Read Ezekiel 3:18-21.

# The
# Requirement

# CHAPTER 4

# IDENTIFYING
# THE CALL

When you begin to experience and encounter things in your life's journey in the Spirit man that can be so detrimental along the way and being in the midst of danger that is seen and unseen, that can often be a matter of life or death. You begin to cry out for help from the depths of your soul with a groaning that only the Spiritual man knows about. You really cannot explain or really understand at the time because it only comes through experiences and encounters with God, and He delivers you from them all.

You will have such a burden and a passion that sometimes can be unbearable, and only you and God will be able to identify and know through Spiritual discernment, "This is what I have really been called to do." You will begin to have the passion and desire to always pray, no matter the time or place. It becomes a part of your character and not only for yourself but even more so on behalf of others, (Prayer becomes your lifestyle). You have dedicated your life to prayer and fasting.

## How to Identify the Call to Prophetic Intercession?

Prophetic intercession can be identified in a combination of reoccurring events. Prophetic intercessors are **awakened with burning to pray on behalf of others** based upon what God has revealed to them. In addition, you will identify the call through a spiritual connection with God through dreams, visions, and personal spiritual encounters.

## Spiritual Connection

You will have that spiritual **connection** with God and a knowing in your spirit man that you have been called to something far greater than you, the ministry of the prophetic. You will begin to seek out the deeper things of God concerning Him and the souls of others with a burning desire from within to intercede. There will be a crying out of travail in your spirit man for them to turn away from a life of sin, shame, and disgrace to be saved.

## Dreams

Through prophetic **dreams,** God will show you about people, places, or events that are happening right now or events happening later. You will be able to identify and know it is truly prophetic when it becomes a reality because everything comes to pass from the dreams. It will also be confirmed and the purpose of it will be revealed.

## Visions

Through open **visions,** you will actually see God performing His word through the revelation of it because it is already happening right before your very eyes. You will see the manifestations of it operating according to how He has spoken and revealed it unto you. God always reveals His word through prophecy and revelation through the spiritual eyes.

## Personal Spiritual Encounters

You will have spiritual **encounters** where you are dealing with demonic forces and attacks where things are coming against you in every area of your life. At times, it can be so detrimental and devastating when you don't know if you are going to make it. You will experience the mercy and the grace of God as you are going through all of this and realize He is the one who brought you through it all. You will know that He is calling you to a place of intercession against spiritual wickedness.

When you have identified that you have the call of

prophetic intercession on your life through the desire to pray for others, your spiritual connection with God, dreams, visions, and personal encounters, it's your responsibility to act on it. This is where you must make the decision to surrender to the call or live a life of disobedience unto God. Understand, no matter what decision you make, God will hold you accountable for fulfilling your purpose.

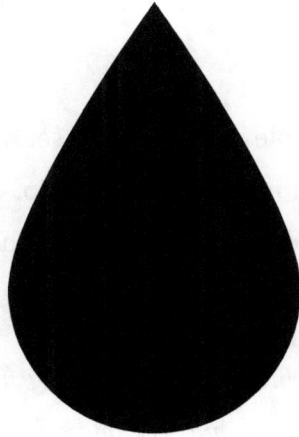

SURRENDERING

TO THE CALL

Once you have recognized there is a prophetic intercession call on your life, you must surrender to it. Surrendering to the call is vitally important to the lives attached to your calling. Those lives are in need of you to stand in the gap, pray them through, and sound the alarm so their lives will be saved.

## Humility

We must humble ourselves and seek His face and turn from or sins as he has commanded for us to do. We cannot be arrogant and prideful. We can only be used by him with the Spirit of humility according to **2 Chronicles 7:14**

> *"If my people, which are called by my name, shall humble themselves, and pray, and seek my face, and turn from their wicked ways; then will I hear from heaven, and will forgive their sin, and will heal their land."*

## Repentance

We must have a heart and a spirit of repentance daily, so we are in right standing with Him always. Then, we will not be in danger of the judgment no matter what we have done so our prayers will not be hindered. **Acts 3:19 reads,**

> *"Repent ye therefore, and be converted, that your sins may be blotted out, when the times of refreshing shall come from the presence of the Lord."*

## Purging and Purification

There must be purging and purification that we must go through from the inside and out; those things that are dead sins and weights; those things that will hinder us from not being totally healed, delivered, and set free. There are things that are hidden and have taken root deep inside, things we are not aware of. We must be purged from those things so the purification and cleansing process can take place, and we can be made whole and free in Him.

For purging:

*In thy filthiness is lewdness: because I have purged thee, and thou wast not purged, thou shalt not be purged from thy filthiness any more, till I have caused my fury to rest upon thee.*

EZEKIEL 24:13

*The blueness of a wound cleanseth away evil: So do stripes the inward parts of the belly.*

PROVERBS 20:30

For purification:

*Having therefore these promises, dearly beloved, let*

*us cleanse ourselves from all filthiness of the flesh and spirit, perfecting holiness in the fear of God.*

2 CORINTHIANS 7:1

*Purge me with hyssop, and I shall be clean: Wash me, and I shall be whiter than snow.*

PSALMS 51:7

Surrendering to the call is a choice that God leaves up to you. It takes a lifestyle of humility, repentance, purging, and purification, so there will be no hindrance in functioning in the responsibility of the call. When you make the decision to walk in total submission and obedience to His will and His way, that is when you have surrendered and yielded yourself to the call.

# CHAPTER 6

# DEVELOPING THE PROPHETIC INTERCESSOR

## Personal Relationship

a. You must have an **intimate** relationship with God, a one-on-one communication. That means allowing him to love on your mind, body, and soul. It is a total surrender to allow him to heal your emotions, your hurt and pain. You must open your heart and trust the process. We must be open and transparent with Him all the time, no matter how difficult it may seem.

b. You must have **discipline** in your life in order to be effective, which means spending quality time with the Holy Spirit and allowing him to speak and minister to you and forsaking everything else that causes distractions and interference. You must set boundaries and have your priorities in order because he is a God of order. This is how we grow into spiritual maturity in Him.

c. You must have **patience** working in your life, for this comes with experience and it builds your character, working through your imperfections along with **longsuffering.** This can sometimes cause you to give up, but you must fight and pray for the strength of God to help you go through. I know sometimes we don't want to. Then, at other times, we find ourselves complaining.

*"For it is God which worketh in you both to will and to do of his good pleasure. Do all things without murmurings and disputings: that ye may be blameless and harmless, the sons of God, without rebuke, in the midst of a crooked and perverse nation, among whom ye shine as lights in the world;"*

PHILIPPIANS 2:13-15

*"For indeed he was sick nigh unto death: but God had mercy on him; and not on him only, but on me also, lest I should have sorrow upon sorrow."*

PHILIPPIANS 2:27

d. You must have **endurance** to be able to stand during the tough times no matter what comes against you because the storms are going to come. It is the (making and breaking) of your spiritual development.

## Understanding the voice of God

a. We understand God's voice through the **revelation** of his written word. This is the primary way we hear His voice as he reveals things to us and gives us instructions. **Deuteronomy 29:28-29 says,**

*"The secret things belong unto the Lord our God: but those things which are revealed belong unto us and to our children forever, that we may do all the words of this law."*

**b.** Another way we understand God's voice is through his **ministering angels** who are assigned to our lives. They watch over us and protect us. They will aide us in times of trouble and minister to our souls and spirits. They are our own personal messengers. As we look at **Psalm 103:19-20 , we find,**

*"Bless the LORD, ye his angels, that excel in strength, that do his commandments, hearkening unto the voice of his word."*

**c.** In addition, we are able to understand the voice of God through a **spoken word** that he speaks to us directly or through his messengers. According to **2 Timothy 3:16-17 , it states,**

*"All scripture is given by inspiration of God, and is profitable for doctrine, for reproof, for correction, for instruction in righteousness: That the man of God may*

*be perfect, thoroughly furnished unto all good works."*

Through our **dreams and visions,** he brings warning. These may be to enlighten us, to encourage us, or to bring confirmation about things we have been seeking answers for. He shows us our destiny and purpose for life prophetically. This is one way I know you will have a real spiritual awakening and for him to get your attention to draw you closer to him.

**Let's read what scripture says:**

*"Why do you contend with Him? For He does not give an accounting of any of His words. For God may speak in one way, or in another, yet man does not perceive it. In a dream, in a vision of the night, when deep sleep falls upon men, while slumbering on their beds, Then He opens the ears of men, And seals their instruction. In order to turn man from his deed, and conceal pride from man, He keeps back his soul from the Pit, And his life from perishing by the sword."*

JOB 33:13-18 NKJV

We must be sensitive to the Holy Spirit when he is speaking and making sure we are hearing him with clarity and instruction:

# Prayer, Meditation, Fasting, and Studying the Word of God

**Prayer** is the main key component during Intercessory time while we are in our secret place communing with the heavenly father without noise nor disruptions. This is our quiet place, so we are hearing his voice and not distracting voices. Prayer is when he is talking, and we are to be quiet and listen.

**Meditation** is also a key component during intercession. It is when you are still; you are quiet and focused and ready to hear him speak. During this time in our worshipping, we are pouring out and crying out in our Spirit were embracing and receiving the things that He shares with us. During this time, one way He encourages us is through our heavenly language (gift of tongues) that is given unto us by Him as well as in English language.

**Fasting** is a critical component of intercession because we are starving our fleshy man [a spiritual discipline] in order to feed the spirit man that must grow and develop into spiritual maturity. When we do this, we are sacrificing our own selfish ways to develop the ways of Christ, so we can be delivered in every area of our life. It is through fasting that we will receive our breakthroughs.

**Studying the word of God** is important for intercession because it brings you closer and it helps to broaden your understanding for you to gain wisdom and knowledge about his word that will guide you to your calling. Your spirit man must be nurtured and fed through the studying of his word to equip you for the battles you will encounter in your walk of life as an intercessor. We must be rooted and grounded in his word [which is our weapon] when the attacks of the enemy come against us.

## Obedience

**Obedient** to the call of intercession is a prime example of being obedient because it brings us in the alignment of our assignment as being called to be an intercessor. When we are obedient, it prompts us to move and flow in excellence when he speaks a command in our spirit. It's at that moment we begin to move and operate in the spirit of obedience in the power and anointing of God.

## Cultivate the Fruit of the Spirit

We are required to walk in the fruit of the Spirit in order to be effective in the ministry we were called to in this hour. As Galatians chapter 5 reads:

*"But the fruit of the Spirit is love, joy, peace, longsuffering, gentleness, goodness, faith, Meekness, temperance: against such there is no law"*

GALATIANS 5:22-23

His **love (agape),** which is his perfect **love,** cast out all fear, and we are to walk in the Spirit each day and show compassion one to another because of his unconditional **love** for us. We are to **love** and forgive no matter who has wronged us and remain in his **love.** For God sacrificed his only son Jesus. Through him, we are saved and have everlasting life.

*"For God so loved the world, that he gave his only begotten Son, that whosoever believeth in him should not perish, but have everlasting life"*

JOHN 3:16

His **joy** is **[unspeakable]** something that is so sweet, and it will make your life complete and full. When you have the **joy** of the Lord, it's going to manifest from the inside out. You can be in a storm, and no one will ever know you're going through unless you allow it to show on the outside through your facial expressions, your attitude, or being angry with the whole world just because you're in a storm. That's not walking in his **joy**. We are to rejoice no matter what the affliction, amen. Why? Let's look at these 2 books 1 Thessalonians 1:6 & 1 John 1:4.

*"And ye became followers of us, and of the Lord, having received the word in much affliction, with joy of the Holy Ghost:"*

1 THESSALONIANS 1:6

*"And these things write we unto you, that your joy may be full."*

1 JOHN 1:4

So according to his word when we're following Christ, we are going to encounter affliction or hardship, but we are to endure these things in joy because it is our strength, and he will make our joy full. Amen "Glory to His name."

His **peace** allows us to rest in him. We don't worry. We don't fret, but we can find comfort in despair when walking in the **peace** of God. Sometimes we can be in turmoil, but only he will give us that blessed assurance that everything is going to be alright. He will speak a word to our heart to encourage us as Philippians chapter 4 says:

*"And the peace of God, which passeth all*

*understanding, shall keep your hearts and minds through Christ Jesus."*

So, he instructs us on how to abide in his **peace** which passeth all understanding when circumstances arise and tries to disrupt our **peace.** We just must do our part and just keep our minds on him Amen "Glory to God."

We must go through the **longsuffering** in order to develop our character to be strong soldiers in his army. Remember the things Christ suffered for us up to his crucifixion right here on earth. He never murmured or complained. He always prayed and asked the father to help him to go through it.

We often don't want to go through the sufferings because we're impatient. We show this through our intolerance or our temper, just to name a few. We just want the easy way out and want the Lord to remove it, but it is the making and the molding of us to be like him. **Longsuffering** is our character builder "Yes, Lord." It matures us into the things of God, and it helps us to appreciate and to be grateful for everything he has done for us, and it brings us to a place of repentance and forgiveness:

*"The LORD is longsuffering, and of great mercy,*

*forgiving iniquity and transgression, and by no means*
*clearing the guilty, visiting the iniquity of the fathers*
*upon the children unto the third and fourth generation."*

NUMBERS 14:18

His **gentleness** is so important to walk in the fruit of the Spirit. We should be calm and not harsh to one another when speaking but we are to respect, honor, and care about each other and speak the truth in love. Let's look at some passages of scriptures in the bible:

*"A soft answer turneth away wrath: but grievous*
*words stir up anger."*

PROVERBS 15:1

*"A wholesome tongue is a tree of life: but perverseness*
*therein is a breach in the spirit."*

PROVERBS 15:4

So, we must be mindful that we don't approach people in the wrong way, even when you are bringing correction and rebuke. We must use wisdom and knowledge on what and how we are relating to someone, and we must be humble in Spirit and not puffed up in arrogance so that it does not cause a reproach on your ministry that you are called to do. We are to speak life and build up, not tear down. As His ministers, we are to bring them to Christ by being gentle with their soul, amen, praise God!!!

We experience his **goodness** through his grace and mercy toward us, not because we have done everything right, but because of His grace. We are saved so that we can live a righteous life and do the work of the ministry that we have been called to do. We are to show that same **goodness** to others as he showed to us in the word:

> *"Withhold not good from them to whom it is due, when it is in the power of thine hand to do it."*

PROVERBS 3:27

This scripture is saying when you see someone in need, help them out and show some compassion. Don't be selfish and inconsiderate and just think about yourself, especially when you have the power to do so. We have to also show goodness even to those who have wronged us. Yes, we must do this if we want to experience his goodness all the days of our lives as Psalms 23:6 says:

> *"Surely goodness and mercy shall follow me    all the days of my life: and I will dwell in the house of the LORD forever."*

We are to walk by faith and not by sight. We must believe that he is going to come through for us no matter what we encounter in life. Sometimes our faith can be shaken from the issues of life, but if we stand firm on his word and seek His face, He will sustain us while our faith is being tested and tried. We are renewed day by day so we cannot lose faith. We have to trust Him.

> *"For which cause we faint not; but though our outward man perish, yet the inward man is renewed day by day."*
>
> 2 CORINTHIANS 4:16

God performed many miracles because he walked the life of **faith** on earth. Just to name a few, here are some scripture references:

**Luke 8: 42 48** - Woman with the issue of blood

**John 2:1 11** - Changing water into wine at Cana

**John 6:16 24** - Jesus walking on water

**John 9: 1 7** - Healing the blind man from birth

We are to exercise our **faith** in order to grow in the **faith** of God which is a daily process because **faith** without works is dead.

*"Yea, a man may say, 'Thou hast faith, and I have works: shew me thy faith without thy works, and I will shew thee my faith by my works.'"*

JAMES 2:18

The Spirit of **meekness** is about the same as being humble and having the Spirit of humility. We are to be lowly in spirit, meaning to be mild-mannered and not loud or boastful. We are to be concerned about the welfare of others and not just about ourselves. If someone is going through and it is affecting their walk with Christ, we who are spiritual are to pray for God to restore such a one back unto Him in the Spirit of meekness as the scripture says:

*"Brethren, if a man be overtaken in a fault, ye which are spiritual, restore such a one in the spirit of meekness; considering thyself, lest thou also be tempted."*

GALATIANS 6:1

Walking in the Spirit of **meekness** is being obedient. This is beautiful in the sight of the Lord. We will experience favor in our lives as Matthew 5 says:

"Blessed are the meek, for they shall inherit the earth."

MATTHEW 5:5

Walking in **temperance** is an important fruit of the Spirit because we must have self-control and discipline over our flesh. The word tells us there is no good thing that dwells in our flesh as we look at Romans 7:21-24

> *"I find then a law, that, when I would do good, evil is present with me. For I delight in the law of God after the inward man: But I see another law in my members, warring against the law of my mind, and bringing me into captivity to the law of sin which is in my members. O wretched man that I am! who shall deliver me from the body of this death?"*

Therefore, we must put our flesh under subjection because we are to walk in the Spirit so that we won't fulfill its lusts. We are to kill our flesh daily. That means to starve it from what it wants and desires and seek God's face for deliverance, amen. We must realize that we cannot just serve him like we want to. As ministers of the gospel, we're held accountable as the scripture says in 1 Corinthians 9:27

> *"But I keep under my body and bring it into subjection: lest that by any means, when I have preached to others, I myself should be a castaway."*

We don't want to be in trouble with God, be done away

with, and be in danger of his judgment. Therefore, it is critical that we walk in the Spirit of **temperance** in this hour, amen.

# CHAPTER 7

# HANDLING THE OPPOSITION WITH THE CALL

# Internal Spiritual Warfare

**Internal Spiritual Warfare** is when we have real personal issues we battle within our (flesh). These are issues we really don't want to deal with or the pain that is associated with it. These struggles can cause us to not live our life to the fullness with Christ, the life He has ordained for us to live. These things can cause us to be emotionally, physically, and spiritually unhealthy and unfit. They can hinder our walk with God. The battle from within may be depression, oppression, fear, rejection, loneliness, hopelessness, lack of faith, lack of confidence, insecurities, low self-esteem, anger, pride, arrogance, unforgiveness, and bitterness. When these things take root, our character becomes contaminated, and we live in self-denial and hide behind a mask that steals our true identity in Christ. We want to believe everything is alright. In reality, we're miserable on the inside, and either we really don't want to deal with the truth, or we don't know how to deal with the truth. When we don't deal with these things, it will cause separation from God because of rebellion against Him, which will lead us to sin.

**As 2 Corinthians 10:3-4 — 5-6** says,

*"We are to cast down these strongholds that will cause*

*us to be disobedient to God and to be free from within and not be held captive in our minds."*

Remember, the **fleshly man** is at war with the **spiritual man,** and no good thing dwells within our flesh, so it must come subject in order for us to walk in the spirit of God:

*"For though we walk in the flesh, we do not war after the flesh: (for the weapons of our warfare are not carnal, but mighty through God to the pulling down of strong holds;) casting down imaginations, and every high thing that exalteth itself against the knowledge of God, and bringing into captivity every thought to the obedience of Christ; 6 and having in a readiness to revenge all disobedience, when your obedience is fulfilled."*

2 CORINTHIANS 10:3-6

In order for us to overcome these things to be effective in Christ:

a.  We must acknowledge that we're battling with these issues, stop the denial, and accept that we need help.

b.  We must seek out wise, spiritual counsel, someone who knows and understands the principles of God.

This must also be someone who will pray and help mentor you through the process to discover the root cause of the issue and teach you how to overcome your struggles.

c.  We must repent and ask God for forgiveness for being rebellious, disobedient, and for allowing those things to enter our hearts and minds, which caused us to sin against Him.

d.  We are to live a life dedicated unto Christ as He has instructed. Prayer and fasting helps us to overcome the spiritual warfare that is to come. This is part of the process of cultivating our character in preparation for the warfare.

e.  We have to learn how to overcome no matter what we are battling with in order to be effective in our call as an intercessor.

## External Spiritual Warfare

**External Spiritual Warfare** is when we battle with things that people try to do against us for various reasons and because of the righteousness of God. These attacks will try to destroy our character and bring discouragement to make us lose focus and abort our assignment. We are going to come against things such as persecution, deception, backbiting, lying, cheating, seductive spirits, abuse, jealousy, hatred, envy, strife, false accusations, slander, and confusion. Sometimes it can also bring on death.

In order for us to overcome these things to be effective in our walk with God:

a.  We must repent and ask God to search our hearts, cleanse us from all unrighteousness, and create in us a clean heart and renew the right spirit within us because it starts with us first.

b.  We must acknowledge and truly know were under attack by way of discernment through the Holy Spirit.

c.  We can seek wise spiritual counsel of someone who knows and understands the principles of God, one who can teach you how to warfare in the spirit through prayer.

d.  We must take power and authority over our battles against the enemy of this world. We are to stand firm in the word of God as our weapon and allow Him to fight for us. We don't always have to speak in the midst of the battle but just live in the peace of God.

I am reminded of when I was going through spiritual warfare at my workplace and I was under great attack coming from every direction. I was on assignment and was capable of doing the work. I was very professional in what I did, and I got it done when I was supposed to. However, because of the jealousy, envy, strife, and other things that manifested against me, I had to go into my secret place of prayer by the water. It is such a peaceful place where me and God had conversations during my breaks and lunch time. He spoke to me and said, "Peace Be Still." At that moment, a Spirit of peace came upon me, and He was assuring me that everything was going to be alright. Not long after that conversation with God, in 1-2 weeks, I began to see things shifting around me, not just in my area but the whole environment. He began to move on my behalf. So, I praise Him for fighting my battles during spiritual warfare. Glory To God!!

> *"And when he was entered into a ship, his disciples followed him. And, behold, there arose a great tempest in the sea, insomuch that the ship was covered with the waves: but he was asleep. And his disciples came to him, and awoke him,*

*saying, Lord, save us: we perish. And he saith unto them, 'Why are ye fearful, O ye of little faith?' Then, he arose and rebuked the winds and the sea; and there was a great calm. But the men marvelled, saying, 'What manner of man is this, that even the winds and the sea obey him!'"*

MATTHEW 8:23-27

We have to believe that God will bring us through our storms and not worry or fret, even though it may seem difficult at times. We may not always see it at the moment, but we have to trust God, have faith, and not fear. He will calm the seas in our lives.

We as intercessors, prophetic intercessors, spiritual gatekeepers, and spiritual watchmen have been commissioned by God to stand in the gap on behalf of others. We must heed to the call in humble submission and obedience in order to fulfill our Kingdom assignments on earth. We must be equipped and able to function in our God ordained positions, effectively and strategically through the operations and leading of the Holy Spirit by flowing in the power and the anointing of God. We must maintain Godly principles and always walk in the spirit of integrity while we are leading by example and reaching the lost at any cost. This must be done so we are not in danger of being judged in our own unrighteousness. We must stand firm on the word of God without compromising the truth and showing compassion one to another by walking in the spirit of love and humility. This is a clarion call to intercession.

# A MESSAGE TO THE PROPHETIC INTERCESSORS

❧ ❦

Just know that if God has called you to the ministry of a prophetic Intercessor, He has already equipped you and qualified you to do it. You only need to humble yourself and surrender unto Him the "YES, LORD." God will bring you to it (allow things to be), and he is more than capable of taking you through it (the test and trials). God will bring you through many encounters where demonic forces try to attack and kill you in the natural and in your dreams. They will also attempt to break your spirit man because of what is destined inside of you. These demonic forces already know what you're capable of, so they will try to stop the process of your life. How do I know? I am a witness. When you begin to have real encounters with demon spirits coming against you, it is real. Just know He has equipped and qualified you to overcome and fight against these evil forces so that His purpose can be fulfilled through your life.

*"Now may the God of peace who brought up our*
*Lord Jesus from the dead, that great Shepherd of the*
*sheep, through the blood of the everlasting covenant,*

*[21] make you complete in every good work to do His will, working in you what is well pleasing in His sight, through Jesus Christ, to whom be glory forever and ever, amen."*

HEBREWS 13:20-21 NKJV

Often, we run from God instead of running to God, especially when He is calling us to do His will. We resist and pull back instead of being obedient and submissive to His way. When that happens, we find ourselves being in calamity because of our disobedience. God wants our total surrender to use us as His vessel so the work of the ministry can be carried out for the Kingdom of God, to tear down the works of darkness here on earth.

**Prayer**

"Oh God, we thank and praise You for who You are in our lives. We give You glory and honor for just being a magnificent God that loves us so unconditionally despite our ways. I ask that you speak to the hearts and minds of your people right now and give them clarity and instructions on what they should be doing in this hour and season concerning you.

I pray that you will no longer allow them to procrastinate, be confused, nor waste time because the time is now to get in a hurry. You are soon to come for your church because we don't want to be left behind and be in danger of your judgment. As this book is opened by every reader, I pray it brings conviction, touches their heart, and transforms their minds right where they are, all over this nation and world. I pray it reveals to them the truth about their identity of who they really are in the ministry of the prophetic, so they can stand in the holy boldness and the righteousness of you. And it is so in the Mighty Name of Jesus, Amen and Amen."

**Prophetess Terri O Anderson**

# ABOUT THE AUTHOR

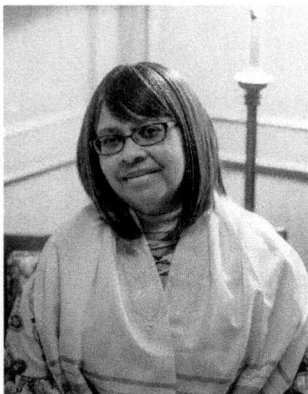

Prophetess Terri O. Anderson, Kingdom Encourager, was born and raised in Indianapolis, IN under the spiritual leadership of the late, great Prophet Joe Anderson and Evangelist/Mother Clara B. Anderson founders of Christian Redemption Church. At the age of 12, she discovered her passion for singing gospel music at her family's church as a psalmist. This opportunity led her to singing with several groups, choirs, and with well-known local gospel artist throughout her life where she received awards and recognitions.

Later, God led her to other ministry assignments, and throughout her journey, she always encouraged and inspired others along the way through her praying, singing, preaching, teaching, and prophecy. God sent her to dark places in her life of ministry to uproot and tear down where the walls of wickedness dwelled. She held Bible study and water baptism in her home. As a result, lives were changed, and many received the gift of the Holy Spirit. During this time of her life, God led her into the ministry of the prophetic and apostolic movement where she received her calling as a prophetic intercessor while going through many spiritual encounters.

On September 29, 2018, Prophetess Anderson received her certificate of ministerial studies from Kingdom Strategist University and became an ordained minister under Divine Order Restoration Ministries International under the leadership of the founder Kingdom Strategist Dr. Derashay. Prophetess Anderson is the founder of Woman of Travail Ministry International which was birthed on November 10, 2018 through Divine Order Restoration Ministries International. The foundation of The Woman Of Travail Ministry International is intercessory prayer and worship according to (Isaiah 56:7). Healing, deliverance, restoration, and the purpose of God is birthed in the lives of the people as she teaches, preaches, and trains through the word of God. Prophetess Terri Anderson is a singer/songwriter and the CEO/President of Anderson Entertainment record label where God allowed her to release two gospel singles in 2020 "Your Majesty" and "Send Your Rain," which were birthed through Woman of Travail Ministry International. The purpose of her music ministry is to bring healing, deliverance and restoration that encourages, transforms, and touches the lives of people all over the world.

## Contact Information

Email Address: wot.ministryinternational@gmail.com

www.ingramcontent.com/pod-product-compliance
Lightning Source LLC
LaVergne TN
LVHW052038080426
835513LV00018B/2373